HOW TO STAY SANE WHILE ROBOTS EAT YOUR JOB

HOW TO STAY SANE WHILE ROBOTS EAT YOUR JOB

THE ART of STAYING HUMAN in an AUTOMATED WORLD

Angelo Alfano, FNP, PMHNP

HOW TO STAY SANE WHILE ROBOTS EAT YOUR JOB

The ART of STAYING HUMAN in an AUTOMATED WORLD
By Angelo Alfano, PMHNP, FNP

First Edition
Copyright © 2026 by Angelo Alfano, PMHNP, FNP

Published by
Rowan and Rye Press

This book is for informational and educational purposes only. The author and publisher make no representations or warranties regarding the accuracy, applicability, or completeness of the contents. The reader assumes full responsibility for their decisions and outcomes based on the information provided.

AI induced Stress Syndrome™ (AISS) is a trademark of Angelo Alfano.

For permission requests, contact MunnAvenuePress.com

Paperback ISBN: 978-1-969679-23-0
Hardcover ISBN: 978-1-969679-24-7

Printed in the United States of America

Important Information from the Author

Before we get started, a quick but important reality check—delivered with care.

Mental health issues are real. Depression, anxiety, trauma, addiction, burnout, and the full constellation of human psychological suffering are not character flaws or personality traits. They are medical and psychological conditions that deserve thoughtful evaluation, evidence-based treatment, and—when appropriate—professional support.

» This book is not a replacement for therapy.

» It is not a substitute for psychiatric care.

» It is not a stand-in for medication when medication is clinically indicated.

» What it is meant to be is context.

I wrote this book as a psychiatric nurse practitioner who spends his days listening to real people describe what it feels like to live inside modern life—burned out, overwhelmed, anxious, numb, and quietly terrified that they're falling behind in a world that won't slow down. Much of what you'll read here reflects patterns I see clinically, interpreted through research, experience, and a strong belief that humor can coexist with seriousness when used responsibly.

You'll encounter frameworks, language, coping tools, and ideas that may help you better understand what's happening in your own mind—or at least feel less alone while it's happening. You may recognize yourself in these pages. You hopefully feel some relief.

That's good.

But if your symptoms are severe, worsening, or interfering with your ability to function—if you're experiencing persistent depression, panic, intrusive thoughts, substance use concerns, thoughts of harming yourself, or a sense that you're barely holding things together—this book is not enough. And it's not supposed to be.

In those situations, the right next step is not another chapter. It's a conversation with a licensed professional—whether that's a therapist, psychiatrist, primary care clinician, or another qualified mental health provider who can evaluate your specific situation and recommend appropriate treatment.

Think of this book the way you'd think of a well-informed friend who knows a lot about psychology, cares deeply about your well-being, and can help you make sense of the chaos—but who would still absolutely insist you see a professional if something serious was going on. Because that's the responsible move. Always.

If at any point while reading this book you find yourself thinking, "This feels bigger than me," please treat that thought not as a failure, but as useful data. Reaching out for help is not an admission of weakness—it's a skill. One that works.

Finally, if you're in immediate danger or thinking about harming yourself or someone else, stop reading and seek emergency help right away. Call your local emergency number, contact a crisis line, or reach out to someone who can be with you in real time. This book will still be here later.

Alright. Paperwork complete. Humanity intact.

Let's get started.

CHAPTER SUMMARIES

Chapter 1: Welcome to the Disruption

Introduces the emotional and psychiatric challenges of living through rapid AI-driven societal change.

Chapter 2: Your Brain on Burnout

Explores the neurobiology and psychological toll of modern burnout, amplified by technological overload.

Chapter 3: The AI Took My Job and My Will to Live

Focuses on the psychological impact of job loss and identity collapse in the AI economy.

Chapter 4: Doomscrolling and Dopamine

Examines the addictive relationship between tech, media consumption, and mental decline.

Chapter 5: From Coping to Margarita

Discusses substance use as a common but dysfunctional coping strategy during times of instability.

Chapter 6: Children of the Disruption

Outlines strategies for raising emotionally resilient children in an unpredictable AI-influenced world.

Chapter 7: Cognitive-Behavioral Therapy (CBT) Tools That Actually Work

Presents proven cognitive behavioral techniques for stress, anxiety, and adaptation.

Chapter 8: Still Mode, Activated

Rebrands meditation and mindfulness in a grounded, BS-free way for the skeptical reader.

Chapter 9: Outrun the Existential Dread

Ties physical movement to emotional and cognitive resilience with science-backed support.

Chapter 10: Upgrade Complete

Offers a roadmap for financial, emotional, and community-based preparation in a changing world.

CHAPTER 1

Welcome to the Disruption

I'm a psychiatric nurse practitioner. That means I spend most of my days talking with real people about real problems, not the pretend kind you solve by yelling at customer service or having a stiff drink. I work in a clinic where emotional breakdowns are common, and the issues people face are hard to imagine. Lately, though, I've noticed something different. Something heavier. Something sharp-edged and ambient—like dread left out overnight.

Over the past few months, I've seen a surge in anxiety, depression, disorientation, and a particularly pungent flavor of existential crisis. And while plenty of that can be chalked up to our current political chaos, it doesn't explain all of it. There's a deeper, stranger tremor running through people. It's not just about the present time; it's about the next thing. The inevitable thing. The "Oh God, I just got replaced by a robot" thing.

That thing is Artificial Intelligence, commonly known as AI.

I've never been a total doomsayer. I see the good in AI, the potential to cure disease, make life easier, and advance technology. I also see the deeply stupid, the wildly irresponsible, and the economically catastrophic. I'm a realist—the kind who drinks strong coffee, reads clinical journals, and occasionally stares into the distance, wondering what happens to therapists when a language model starts giving relationship advice that actually works.

This book is my attempt to offer something useful before the next wave hits. A little scaffolding. A few handholds. A survival manual for the psyche, duct-taped together with clinical research, a handful of therapeutic tools, and just enough sarcasm to keep you from screaming into the void.

Because make no mistake—change is coming. And it's not going to be a gentle nudge. It's a stick of dynamite wrapped in a TED Talk. AI will rewrite the rules of work, identity, and connection, exploding long-held assumptions in the process. As economist Erik Brynjolfsson warned, "AI won't just replace jobs — it will transform them, forcing us to rethink what it means to be valuable in the workplace." The shift isn't theoretical. It's already happening.

What I hope to do in the pages ahead is help you stay human while all of that happens. Not perfect. Not enlightened. Just grounded, resilient, and maybe laughing a little as the algorithms tighten their grip.

We'll walk through the tools to help you stay sane—real ones, not the kind you get from an Instagram reel promising "10 hacks to inner peace," but actual cognitive frameworks, body-based practices, and a few psychological crowbars for prying yourself off the floor. And through it all, I'll try to keep it honest, useful, and just dark enough to make your therapist nervous. As I often tell my patients: Laughter isn't the best medicine, but it *is* a controlled substance, and I'm fully licensed to prescribe it off-label.

THE AI AVALANCHE: WHAT'S COMING

Artificial Intelligence has arrived—not just as a helpful assistant that alphabetizes your bookshelf, but as a cheerfully tireless overachiever who doesn't take lunch breaks, doesn't call in sick, and is surprisingly okay with stealing your job. It's not evil. It's just ... efficient and immune to hangovers. Like a polite Terminator that can also manage your stock portfolio.

In the beginning, it was cute. AI wrote poems, made mediocre art, and was occasionally responsible for crashing a car. But now? It edits films, controls drone strikes, gives investment advice, and just casually passed the California State Bar Exam. Meanwhile, you're struggling to figure out how to download the new Netflix app on your cell phone and still have not started learning Spanish for the tenth year in a row.

Let's not pretend this is just a technical evolution. It's a psychological unmooring. Every time your newsfeed mentions another AI breakthrough, a tiny part of your ego quietly packs a box, clears its desk, and gets in line for unemployment benefits.

And if you're a professional in a knowledge-based industry—lawyer, therapist, writer, teacher—AI isn't just encroaching on your job. It's doing it without complaining about time off or insurance premiums and with better punctuation and zero emotional baggage.

Dario Amodei, CEO of Anthropic, warns that AI could eliminate up to 50 percent of entry-level white-collar jobs within the next five years, potentially pushing U.S. unemployment rates to 20 percent.[1]

THE HUMAN RESPONSE: ANXIETY AND EXISTENTIAL DREAD

You may already be coping in familiar ways. Coffee. More coffee. Passive-aggressive Teams messages. Taller glasses of bourbon. Hobby hoarding. And yes, it's funny. Until it's not. Until your identity, which has been braided into your profession, starts fraying. Until you're arguing with a chatbot about your own medical diagnosis. Until the job you trained for most of your life becomes an optional side feature of a productivity algorithm.

IBM reports that more than 120 million workers globally will need retraining in the next three years due to artificial intelligence's impact on jobs.[2]

So, how do we stay sane? Short answer: we don't, not fully. Long answer: we learn new tools. We adapt. And we get better at laughing inappropriately at precisely the right time. The name of the game is resilience; some of us have it, most

1 Thomas Barrabi, "AI Could Spark Bloodbath for White-Collar Jobs — and Send Unemployment to 20%: Anthropic CEO," New York Post, May 28, 2025, https://nypost.com/2025/05/28/business/ai-could-cause-bloodbath-for-white-collar-jobs-spike-unemployment-to-20-anthropic-ceo/.

2 Shelly Hagan, "Robots Displacing Jobs Means 120 Million Workers Need Retraining," Bloomberg News, September 6, 2019, 2 https://www.bloomberg.com/news/articles/2019-09-06/robots-displacing-jobs-means-120-million-workers-need-retraining.

of us don't, but we could all use an upgrade.

CLINICAL INSIGHT: UNDERSTANDING THE PSYCHOLOGICAL IMPACT

Let's switch hemispheres—from right-brain panic to left-brain analysis. Humans are evolutionarily wired for three things: predictability, connection, and competence. AI threatens all three at once. This isn't burnout from working too hard. It's burnout from feeling replaceable in a system you don't fully understand and have no control over.

In psychological terms, what we're experiencing is anticipatory grief. It's the sense of loss before loss occurs. You're grieving a future self who might not matter the way you do now. When the things we value are made redundant—contribution, creativity, and stability—so is the meaning we've attached to them.

And it doesn't stop at work. AI-fueled disruption is making guest appearances in our relationships, our confidence, and even how we parent. It's hard to feel like a present, tuned-in caregiver when your kid's tablet knows their favorite bedtime story, snack, and attention span better than you do. Welcome to modern life, where even the robots have opinions on screen time.

AI-INDUCED STRESS SYNDROME: A PROPOSED DIAGNOSTIC FRAMEWORK[3]

It's time we name what's happening.

AI-Induced Stress Syndrome (AISS) is not yet a formally recognized psychiatric diagnosis, but the psychological

---

3 AI induced Stress Syndrome™ (AISS) is a trademark of Angelo Alfano.

manifestations are becoming difficult to ignore. Clinically, it could be conceptualized as an emerging adjustment disorder subtype, characterized by persistent anxiety, anticipatory grief, and occupational identity disruption in response to accelerated technological displacement. Adjustment disorder is basically what happens when life throws you a curveball and your brain hasn't quite figured out how to swing at it. The stress hits harder than you expected and instead of bouncing back, it sticks.

Core symptom domains might include:

» Affective dysregulation—including chronic anxiety, irritability, or apathy related to automation or job instability

» Cognitive intrusions—recurring thoughts about redundancy, self-worth in a digitized economy, or being replaced by algorithms

» Behavioral shifts—such as compulsive upskilling, doomscrolling, withdrawal from professional social networks, or avoidance of emerging technologies

» Somatic indicators—including sleep disturbance, muscle tension, and digital fatigue (e.g., screen-related eyestrain, phantom notifications)

From a psychiatric perspective, AISS reflects the collision of rapid external change with the brain's slower adaptive capacity. We are witnessing an environmental stressor that is ambient, chronic, and often intangible—a kind of low-frequency existential hum disrupting the usual rhythms of self-regulation.

If you've found yourself yelling at a chatbot, questioning

your relevance mid-Zoom call, or quietly hoping your company's AI rollout crashes just long enough for you to keep your health insurance—congratulations, you may be experiencing a textbook case of AISS.

Other signs include:

» Emotional numbness when your job title appears in a product demo
» A sudden urge to learn Python at 2 a.m.
» Developing a sudden, unexplainable interest in homesteading

The bad news: the robots are real. The good news: so are you. And unlike them, you have the uniquely human ability to adapt with humor, resilience, and the occasional full-system meltdown.

Let's not just cope. Let's recalibrate. Because while AI may be optimizing the world, your job is to stay human in it—and that, it turns out, is still a competitive advantage. What to do? We adapt. We're entering an age where cognitive overload isn't an emergency, it's just Monday. Emotional dysregulation? That's no longer a red flag, it's a personality trait. And attention spans? They're about as reliable as group texts with your extended family—fractured, scattered, and somehow always missing the point.

We bounce between tabs, tasks, and existential dread like caffeinated hamsters on a wheel we paid $11.99/month to subscribe to. Our brains weren't built for this kind of input; they were built to scan for saber-toothed tigers, not respond to Slack, Tinder, DoorDash, and a breaking news alert about the collapse of democracy in the same minute

The good news: you can still respond. Not with

denial—that market's saturated—but with strategy. This book isn't just a warning siren; it's a field guide for staying human in a Techno revolution.

Inside, you'll learn how to decatastrophize, meditate without needing a Himalayan salt lamp or a trust fund, reprogram your stress response, and quite literally sweat your way to mental clarity. These aren't magic spells or Instagram affirmations—they're evidence-based interventions, just dressed in black humor and written without the clinical fine print.

If you're here for crystal chakra downloads or recommendations for coffee colonics, you're going to be disappointed. But if you're trying to reboot your sanity between doomscrolling sessions, if you want to stay grounded during this shift, you're in the right place.

Because here's the part most people forget in all this noise: The human condition has always been built for chaos. We evolved through scarcity, disaster, uncertainty, and wild guesses. This isn't new—it's just faster and better lit. Yes, the tools are changing. Yes, the pressure is on. But you are still, at your core, a deeply adaptive, wired-for-survival, storytelling machine. That's your edge.

You're not just a passenger on this ride. You're still holding the wheel—even if it feels like it's occasionally spinning out of control.

So no, we can't stop the world from changing. But we can choose how we meet that change—with clarity, humor, grit, and maybe just enough irreverence to stay sane. That's what this book is about: keeping humanity intact while the algorithms try to optimize it out of you.

Let's begin.

CHAPTER 2

*Why you forgot what you were doing five seconds ago,
and how to stop yelling at your toaster*

It starts with a headline.

"Goldman Sachs Predicts 300 Million Jobs Will Be Impacted by AI.[4]"

You scroll past it, vaguely nauseated, thumb twitching. You're not Goldman Sachs. You're not even in sales. You're a copywriter, a therapist, an accountant, a radiologist, a teacher—hell, maybe even a truck driver trying to keep your benefits long enough to hit retirement. But somewhere deep in the lizard-brain parts of your consciousness, a slow panic takes root. Not all at once. Just enough to make your coffee taste a little off.

Let's begin with a confession: you're not broken. You

---

4 "Goldman Sachs Predicts 300 Million Jobs Will Be Impacted by AI." New York Post, May 28. https://nypost.com/2025/05/28/business/ai-could-cause-bloodbath-for-white-collar-jobs-spike-unemployment-to-20-anthropic-ceo/

are, quite reasonably, exhausted. What's happening to your attention span, your motivation, your sense of meaning—it's not some isolated failure of character. It's burnout, and it's baked into the very operating system of our modern economy. If you've felt like you're running on fumes while trying to outrun a fire you can't quite see, welcome to the club. Membership is free but comes with fatigue, irritability, and an increased risk of screaming into your steering wheel in grocery store parking lots.

Burnout isn't new, but it has evolved. In the age of AI, algorithmic overload, and ambient existential dread, burnout is no longer just a workplace hazard. It's a societal feature. And it's spreading faster than any virus. The usual suspects—capitalism, overwork, tech addiction—have been joined by newer ones: automation anxiety, 24/7 digital surveillance, and the gnawing sense that you're being left behind by a system you never even agreed to participate in.

THE NEW ANATOMY OF BURNOUT

Burnout used to be something you got after 90-hour work weeks in a high-rise or field hospital. Now it's showing up in stay-at-home parents, teenagers, gig workers, and even AI engineers who are, ironically, building the very systems that make everyone else feel obsolete. The symptoms have broadened too, beyond workplace fatigue, into a sense of being existentially flattened.

Clinically, burnout consists of three main ingredients:

1. **Emotional exhaustion**—the tank is empty and no amount of sleep refills it
2. **Depersonalization**—feeling disconnected from

others, cynical, and/or numb

3. **Reduced sense of personal accomplishment—**
you do things, but they feel meaningless

According to the World Health Organization (WHO), burnout is now recognized as a diagnosable occupational phenomenon. But in practice, it leaks into every domain of life. Relationships, parenting, creativity—all become collateral damage when your nervous system is operating in survival mode. Burnout is the body's honest response to dishonest demands.

THE AI MULTIPLIER

Burnout isn't just about working too much—it's about not being allowed to stop. And AI, bless its soulless heart, has made everything faster, more competitive, and more desta-bilizing. You're no longer just trying to finish your to-do list. You're doing that while ChatGPT rewrites résumés in seconds, Midjourney generates art better than you can draw, and LinkedIn profiles brag about nineteen-year-olds who just launched their fourth company and bought an island. Every app on your phone is optimized to hijack your dopa-mine system. Your brain was designed for meaningful social interaction and long-term goals. Instead, it's flooded with micro-distractions, status updates, push notifications, and AI-crafted content that makes you feel obsolete.

"It is no measure of health to be well adjusted to a profoundly sick society."

— **Jiddu Krishnamurti**[5]

---

5 Krishnamurti, Jiddu. The First and Last Freedom. New York: Harper & Brothers, 1954.

We now have a name for this new constellation of stress responses—AISS. It's not just burnout with a tech twist; it's a chronic state of cognitive whiplash triggered by an accelerating world where the benchmarks of success keep shifting and the humans are expected to keep pace with machines.

The net effect is a quiet panic that you're not doing enough, not fast enough, and not unique enough to be worth anything in a world where even the machines are getting promotions.

YOUR BRAIN ON CHRONIC STRESS

Picture your brain as a beautifully tuned orchestra. Now imagine someone lighting the cello on fire while a sleep-deprived oboist is forced to play TikTok jingles during a fire drill. That's your brain on stress. Chronic stress increases cortisol, which impairs the hippocampus (the part responsible for memory and learning), while simultaneously over-activating the amygdala (your panic button). Over time, your prefrontal cortex—the rational part—goes offline more quickly. You become more reactive, less reflective. And this becomes the new normal. A 2018 meta-analysis in *Frontiers in Psychology* confirmed what clinicians have known for years: long-term stress impairs cognitive flexibility, decision-making, and memory.

Translation? You're not losing your mind. You're just exhausted from juggling too much nonsense. Stress makes it harder to prioritize, see the big picture, and access emotional nuance. Everything feels equally urgent—or equally impossible. A perfect example of this was the COVID-19 pandemic. The pandemic didn't just rewrite work—it rewired brains. Since 2020, there's been a marked increase in adult ADHD diagnoses, particularly among women and knowledge workers.

But what we're seeing isn't necessarily a sudden outbreak of previously undetected neurodivergence. It's something more insidious: the cognitive signature of burnout masquerading as a disorder. Research from *JAMA Psychiatry* and *Psychiatric Times* suggests that the spike in ADHD symptoms during COVID correlates more closely with chronic stress, disrupted routines, sleep dysregulation, and emotional exhaustion than with traditional ADHD pathology.[6,7] In essence, when your neural pathways are under siege—from layoffs, remote overload, or existential dread—it starts to look a lot like ADHD. But this isn't a disorder of attention. It's a normal brain adapting to abnormal levels of uncertainty, hypervigilance, and exhaustion. Burnout flattens your mood and fragments your focus. It looks like ADHD, smells like anxiety, and feels like PTSD—it's AISS.

On top of that, your vagus nerve—the system that helps regulate calm—starts to lose tone. This means you're more likely to stay in fight-or-flight mode, even after the email from your boss turns out to be benign. When your vagal tone is low, everything feels like an emergency.

THE CASE OF JORDAN (MY MOST COMMON PATIENT)

Jordan was a pediatric nurse and a parent of two young kids. After the pandemic, she returned to work feeling flat but functional—until she wasn't. She began forgetting small

---

6 Hirshberg, Lawrence M., et al. 2021. "Adult ADHD Diagnoses and Cognitive Patterns in Post-Pandemic Populations." JAMA Psychiatry 78 (5): 432–440.

7 Adler, Larry A., and Thomas J. Spencer. 2023. "Burnout, Executive Dysfunction, and Misdiagnosis: Understanding the ADHD Surge." Psychiatric Times 40 (3): 12–18

things. Coffee left on the roof of the car. Losing her phone in the fridge. Her ability to concentrate dropped. She snapped at her kids, lost patience with patients, and cried when she had to make small talk at work. She thought she was losing it. Her doctor ran labs. Nothing looked wrong. But everything was wrong. She was running on fumes. No fuel, no joy, no vision. Just forward motion because stopping felt scarier. Burnout doesn't always scream. Sometimes it whispers, "Just get through today." And then tomorrow. And then forever. Sound familiar?

WHY REST DOESN'T ALWAYS WORK

You've probably tried resting. Maybe even scheduled a weekend off. But instead of bouncing back, you found yourself doomscrolling, binge-watching, or wondering if it's normal to feel hollow while lying on a beach. Real rest doesn't mean collapsing on the couch with a third margarita and a fourth rerun of a show you've already seen. It means downregulating the nervous system—the parasympathetic "rest and digest" part that got steamrolled by your deadline-obsessed sympathetic system. True rest can be active: a hot bath, yoga, silence, slow walks, breathing deeply with your napping kid on your chest. It can also be creative—journaling, knitting, even reorganizing your garage—if it connects you to rhythm and presence.

> *"Almost everything will work again if you unplug it for a few minutes, including you."*
>
> — Anne Lamott[8]

---

8 Lamott, Anne. *Small Victories: Spotting Improbable Moments of Grace.* New York: Riverhead Books, 2014.

Sometimes you don't need a vacation. You need a new relationship to your own exhaustion.

BURNOUT'S INTERNAL ALGORITHM

Burnout doesn't just fatigue your body. It rewires your inner monologue.

"You're lazy."

"You're behind."

"Everyone else is doing more."

"If you stop, you'll fall apart."

These thoughts don't come from truth—they come from survival mode. And they lie. High performers are especially susceptible. We reward productivity with praise and identity. So, when that engine stalls, the shame sets in. You go from "I can do anything" to "Why can't I get out of bed?" Burnout turns your drive into your prison. You're not exhausted because you're weak. You're exhausted because you've been strong for too long without enough recovery. Now for the good news: Burnout is not a life sentence. Your brain is plastic. Your nervous system is trainable. You are not a lost cause. Burnout thrives on helplessness, so start with micro-wins: brush your teeth, fold two shirts, cancel one meeting, or say "No" just once this week. Each act is a vote for your own autonomy.

But we don't just burn out from overwork—we burn out from underpurpose. Schedule meaning, not just tasks. Put joy in the calendar—not as a chore, but as a right: a bike ride, some kitchen dancing, a quiet moment stargazing. Choose something that asks nothing of you.

Try a guilt-free approach to exercise—mood mobilization

—which encourages nervous system regulation over aesthetics. Walk while listening to birds, stretch and hum, or do five squats and call it resistance training. Just get your blood moving so your brain gets a break. Because *any* exercise is exponentially more beneficial than none. According to the WHO, even small amounts of movement—just ten minutes a day—are linked to lower rates of depression, anxiety, and premature death. You don't have to train for a marathon. You just have to start.

And when it gets hard? That's the point. Movement is practice for life. The first rep, the first step, the first walk around the block when you'd rather crawl into bed—that's where you remind yourself: *I can do hard things.* **The choice isn't between hard and easy. It's between *this kind of hard*—the sweat, the discomfort, the inertia—and *that kind of hard*—the numbness, the panic, the stagnation. You get to choose your hard.**

> *"If you don't pick a day to rest, your body will pick it for you."*
>
> —Unknown (but probably your joints whispering through the pain)

Mood mobilization isn't about sculpting your body into a billboard. It's about reclaiming your agency one movement at a time. Your nervous system will appreciate it. Your anxiety will lower its voice. And your future self will look back and say, "Thank you for getting up when it didn't feel worth it." Try noticing the waves of stress and sticky thoughts; breathe through themt without attaching a story. You'll be amazed at how fast you recover once you stop fueling the fire.

Finally, talk about it. Burnout shrinks in the light. Tell

someone. Start a group. Make it normal to say, "I'm overwhelmed." Connection is medicine.

> *"Between stimulus and response, there is a space. In that space is our power to choose our response."*
> — **Viktor Frankl**[9]

You're not malfunctioning, you're adapting. If you feel scattered, foggy, anxious, or numb, it doesn't mean you're broken. It means your brain is doing its best to survive a world that's changing faster than it can process. That's the core of AISS. It's a very human response to very inhuman conditions. And here's the good news—you still have choices. You can choose to move forward even when it's uncomfortable. You can choose to do hard things, not because you're a machine but because you're not. Your nervous system, your habits, your sense of self—they're all malleable.

This book isn't here to fix you. It's here to remind you that **you still work**, even when the world around you feels like it doesn't. If burnout is a signal that something's out of sync, then recovery begins not with hustle, but with reconnection. And as we'll explore in the next chapter, your attention—fragmented as it may feel—is still yours to reclaim. Let's start there. Back in Chapter 1, we started this journey with a simple premise: Humans are incredibly adaptive. Burnout is not the end of your story. It's the warning sign that your body still believes in your survival.

So let's write the next chapter—not in panic, not in shame, but in the slow, stubborn, beautiful practice of becoming human again.

---

9 Frankl, Viktor E. Man's Search for Meaning. Boston: Beacon Press, 1959.

CHAPTER 3

AI Took My Job and My Will to Live

Why you don't feel crazy for panicking—and how to adapt without fully spiraling.

It starts with a headline. Let's begin with some hard truth wrapped in a tortilla of humor: Yes, the robots are coming. No, you're not being paranoid. And yes, it's totally reasonable to feel a mix of dread, anger, grief, and the unshakable desire to live in a cabin off-grid, eating canned lentils and learning blacksmithing. The rise of AI and automation isn't just an economic disruption—it's a psychological one. And for the first time in human history, we're experiencing what psychologists might call existential displacement: the fear that not only is your *skill set* obsolete, but your *identity* is too.

Remember that caveman part of your brain we met in Chapter 1? It's still looking for saber-toothed tigers. And guess what? They now come in the form of job loss, LinkedIn announcements, and headlines like "AI Outperforms

Doctors in Diagnosis."

This chapter is not about stopping the robots. It's about staying sane while they rearrange the workforce and possibly your life. It's about grief, reinvention, and remembering that humans have survived worse. Black Plague, anyone? So, let's talk about how to adapt like a psychologically resilient cockroach in a rapidly changing machine world.

THE GRIEF OF BEING REPLACED

Losing your job to automation feels like losing a paycheck and the proof of your usefulness. You might tell yourself, "It's just work," but it's never *just* work. Work is identity. Work is structure. Work is the answer to the "What do you do?" question we all receive at awkward weddings. AI doesn't just take jobs. It takes the rituals, the small talk, the office snacks, the casual sense of purpose that come with showing up somewhere and mattering.

> *"The most painful state of being is remembering the future, particularly the one you'll never have."*
> — **Søren Kierkegaard**[10]

That's grief. Not for the past, but for the imagined future you had planned. The title you were working toward. The financial stability. The story you told yourself about who you'd be in five years. And now, it's being rewritten by an algorithm that doesn't need coffee breaks or dental coverage. For many, this loss is silent. There's no funeral for a deleted department. But make no mistake—grief is

---

10 Kierkegaard, Søren. Either/Or: A Fragment of Life. Translated by Alastair Hannay. London: Penguin Classics, 1992.

happening. And unlike conventional loss, there's often no social script to follow. You're expected to "pivot," "upskill," and "remain optimistic," all while your inner compass is spinning wildly.

THE SHAME SPIRAL

Here's the part we don't talk about enough: Getting replaced by a machine can feel deeply shameful. You might start asking questions that spiral inward:

> » If a program can do this, was I ever really that skilled?
> » Why didn't I learn to code earlier?
> » Why does everyone on the Internet seem to be pivoting so smoothly while I'm still in sweatpants Googling "Is philosophy obsolete?"

And then the comparisons start. Everyone on LinkedIn seems to be flourishing in disruption. New titles. New ventures. AI startups. You? You're just trying to make peace with the fact that a chatbot got your job while you were sleeping. This is where shame thrives—in isolation, in silence, in the perceived failure to adapt. But let's be very clear: Your worth is not defined by how automatable you are. You are not a product. You are a person navigating systemic upheaval. That's not a weakness. That's evidence of your humanity.

> *"Life exists only at his very moment, and in this moment it is infinite and eternal."*
> — **Alan W. Watts**[11]

---

11 Watts, Alan W. n.d. Become What You Are.

Your reaction isn't dysfunction. It's data. It's your nervous system telling the truth about what it means to be human in a time of dehumanizing efficiency.

THE BIOLOGY OF ECONOMIC FEAR

Let's talk cortisol. When you lose your job, your nervous system doesn't understand macroeconomics. It thinks you've been cast out of the tribe. And in evolutionary terms, that meant you were about to be eaten by wolves—or slowly freeze while holding a stick. That's not drama. That's neurobiology. Studies show that chronic job insecurity and unemployment correlate with increased rates of depression, anxiety, cardiovascular disease, and even mortality. A 2020 study in *The Lancet Psychiatry* found that unemployment increases suicide risk by 20–30%, especially when paired with financial stress and isolation.

So, if you're overwhelmed, doomscrolling, crying in the bathtub, or losing track of what day it is—it's not just you. It's your body trying to survive perceived extinction. This is why your nervous system needs regulation before reinvention. You can't job-hunt effectively from a state of panic. You need to create safety first—even if that safety is just a daily walk, a cup of tea, or a conversation with someone who gets it. Burnout, anxiety, and executive dysfunction are signs that your brain is attempting to adapt. Just clumsily. Like a toddler trying to put on adult shoes.

THE AI ILLUSION

Here's the twist: AI isn't replacing everyone. It's replacing *tasks*.

But media headlines—and your cousin Chad—are great at

making it sound like entire professions are going extinct. The truth? AI excels at narrow, defined, repeatable processes. It can:

  » Sort data
  » Generate code
  » Automate scheduling
  » Analyze patterns

But it still can't do nuance, empathy, context, humor, or ethical judgment. It can't comfort a grieving parent. It can't brainstorm under pressure. It can't sense tension in a room. It can't understand irony. It can't decide when *not* to act. That means AI is great at efficiency, but terrible at humanity. And if your work requires humanity, you're still needed— *just differently.*

ADAPTATION IS A SKILL, NOT A TRAIT

Some people say, "I'm just not good with change," but like any habit, it can be rewired. Psychological flexibility—the ability to stay present with discomfort and still move in a valued direction—is one of the strongest predictors of long-term resilience. According to Acceptance and Commitment Therapy (ACT), it's not about controlling your thoughts. It's about choosing your behavior in spite of them.

"This is hard. And I can still take the next step."

That's the mantra. That's adaptation in real time.

CHOOSE YOUR HARD (REDUX)

We introduced this idea earlier, but here, it's fully operational:

  » It's hard to be unemployed.
  » It's hard to reinvent yourself.
  » One kind of hard keeps you stuck.

> » The other kind moves you forward—awkwardly and painfully, but forward nonetheless.

Choosing hard doesn't mean *ignoring your emotions*. It means *coexisting with them*. You can grieve *and* write a cover letter. You can panic *and* update your résumé. You can feel broken *and* still apply for that grant, program, or part-time gig that gets you one inch closer to stability. Progress doesn't require clarity. It requires motion.

THE REINVENTION TOOLKIT

Let's get tactical. Psychological reinvention isn't about radical transformation. It's about tiny, consistent acts of agency.

1. Track Your Identity Loss

Write down all the parts of your identity tied to your previous role. Then ask these questions:

> » What did I actually enjoy?
> » What parts were performative?
> » What values remain even if the job is gone?

This is grief work. But it's also design work. You're mourning the old you while sketching the next version.

2. Connect with Others in Transition

You need community. Not just for advice, but for emotional survival. Isolation is a megaphone for despair. Look for spaces—online or in-person—where people are real about what they're facing, not just selling six-figure rebrands.

3. Learn—But Set Boundaries

The instinct to "upskill" is valid. But don't become a

one-person tech bootcamp. Pick a single learning target. Experiment and iterate, but don't forget to rest. You're not a productivity algorithm.

4. Rebuild Routine

Even a loose routine signals to your nervous system that *we're still safe*. Wake up. Move. Eat. Apply. Connect. Repeat. Bonus points if pants are involved.

5. Anchor to Purpose

Right now, your purpose might just be to not spiral. That counts. If you show up for yourself today—messy, imperfect, barely functioning—that's purpose in action. You don't have to be optimized. You just have to be alive.

"BUT WHAT IF THE ROBOTS REALLY DO WIN?"

Maybe they will. Maybe entire industries will be reshaped or disappear. Maybe Universal Basic Income becomes a thing. Maybe capitalism gets an upgrade. Maybe it doesn't. But even in the worst-case scenario, you're not powerless. You can adapt— not because it's easy, but because that's literally what humans do. We've survived climate collapses, empires crumbling, the Internet, and reality TV. We've eaten bugs, invented vaccines, and figured out how to laugh at funerals. This is just another curve. Maybe sharper. Maybe faster. But still survivable.

> *"When we are no longer able to change a situation, we are challenged to change ourselves."*
> — Viktor Frankl[12]

---

12 Frankl, Viktor E. Man's Search for Meaning. Boston: Beacon Press, 1959.

THE FUTURE ISN'T CANCELED—IT'S JUST DIFFERENT

There is life after job loss. There is identity after disorientation. There is dignity in rebuilding. No robot, no algorithm, and no billionaire's chatbot can replicate your story, your lens, your humor, and your humanity. This chapter isn't a call to arms. It's a call to adapt. With intention. With community. With compassion for yourself in the middle of the uncertainty. You're not behind. You're not obsolete. You're a work in messy, glorious progress. Let's move forward—one awkward, rebellious, defiant step at a time.

CHAPTER 4

Doomscrolling and Dopamine

Why your brain is addicted to the apocalypse, and how to outwit your primal wiring in the age of infinite fear.

THERE'S A MOMENT—RIGHT AROUND 11:47 P.M.—WHEN the human spirit is at its weakest. You've brushed your teeth. You've told yourself, earnestly, that tonight's the night you'll get eight hours. You set your phone on the nightstand like it's radioactive. But it's not even a minute before you pick it back up. Just to check something. A quick scroll. Two hours later, you're chest-deep in a Reddit thread on the water wars of 2040, your thumb locked in an involuntary swipe-loop, and your eyes glazed over from a TikTok explaining how microplastics are now detectable in human placentas. You've gone from sleepy to stressed to paranoid to numb, and you still can't stop. Congratulations. You've been doomscrolling.

This chapter is not an intervention. It's a confession. Because we've all done it. And most importantly, your brain is doing exactly what it was designed to do. It's just doing it in a digital hellscape optimized for distraction, fear, and emotional volatility. You're not weak. You're outmatched.

A NERVOUS SYSTEM BUILT FOR TIGERS

To understand doomscrolling, we need to understand the operating system we're running. Your brain—and its ancient dopamine circuitry—was forged in a world of predators and scarcity. It evolved to react quickly to threats, remember bad news, and stay hyper-alert in uncertain conditions. That wiring kept us alive when the threat was a prehistoric predator. Now the tigers are in your pocket, disguised as headlines.

This isn't just a metaphor.

Your limbic system—the emotional part of your brain—lights up when you see a headline about climate collapse or political unrest. Your amygdala, that little almond-shaped alarm bell, doesn't differentiate between an actual threat and a tweet about a threat. It responds the same way: heart rate up, cortisol released, focus narrowed. Fight, flight, or freeze. Or in modern terms: refresh, retweet, repost. Here's the kicker: the dopamine system loves anticipation more than resolution. So even though doomscrolling makes you feel worse, your brain is secretly loving the hunt. That next headline might be the one. The post that explains it all. The reel that finally answers your anxiety with a plan. But it never does. And so, we scroll.

> *"The Internet is the first thing that humanity has built that humanity doesn't understand."*
>
> — Eric Schmidt[13]

---

13 Schmidt, Eric. Quoted in The New Digital Age: Reshaping the Future of People, Nations and Business. By Eric Schmidt and Jared Cohen. New York: Alfred A. Knopf, 2013.

SIMULATED CONTROL, REAL ANXIETY

The most dangerous part of doomscrolling is the illusion. It feels like we're doing something. Like we're preparing, staying ahead, being responsible. But consuming endless information about crises does not translate to action. It translates to paralysis. I've had patients who start their day with a news feed and end it with a panic attack. Who believe they're informed but can't sleep. Who feel guilty if they don't keep up, as if being offline for twelve hours is the moral equivalent of hiding during a house fire. The reality is that our nervous systems were never meant to process the suffering of the entire planet in real time. Let alone during lunch breaks. And yet, our digital world is structured precisely to reward this behavior. The more outrage, fear, and uncertainty you feel, the more engaged you become. The business model of social media is emotional escalation. Your brain is being manipulated by algorithms smarter than any human, and your only real weapon is awareness. So, let's get aware.

THE HIDDEN COST OF INFINITE SCROLLING

What happens when we expose our minds to a twenty-four-hour buffet of worst-case scenarios? Sleep erodes. Decision-making flattens. Anxiety spikes. And perhaps most devastatingly, hope decays. Because doomscrolling trains the brain to expect collapse, to discount nuance, and to believe that no action is worthwhile. You read about the climate crisis, feel overwhelmed, and do nothing. Repeat that loop a thousand times, and your brain learns that nothing can be done. You become emotionally sophisticated in despair and intellectually paralyzed in your own life. I'm not being dramatic. A 2021 study published in *Health Communication* found that "problematic news consumption" was directly correlated with physical ill-being and emotional distress.[14] That's a fancy way of saying: The more you scroll, the worse you feel—and the harder it becomes to stop. It's the perfect trap. But traps can be outsmarted.

INTERRUPTING THE SPELL

Let me tell you about Kevin.

Kevin was a software engineer who came to me with insomnia, panic attacks, and the belief that the world was "on a timer and the buzzer already went off." His sleep was destroyed. His relationships were fraying. He kept doom-scrolling as if it were a moral obligation. Every night, he'd try to stop. Every night, he'd fail. When I asked what he was hoping to find in all his scrolling, he said: "A reason to believe I'm not crazy for feeling this way."

There it was. He wasn't searching for data—he was searching for validation. For community. For proof that his fear was real. We made a deal. For every hour he spent online reading collapse theories, he'd spend ten minutes writing down what he could still control. Not hypotheticals, but actual, concrete actions. Switch to a reusable water bottle. Vote in local elections. Text a friend. Take a walk. It felt ridiculous at first. But something shifted. His brain, used to endless doom spirals, began to rewire toward agency. Toward action. Toward grounded reality.

---

14 Bendau, Antonia, Jonathan Plag, Moritz Wösten, and Andreas Ströhle. 2021. "Problematic News Consumption and Its Association with Mental and Physical Health During the COVID-19 Pandemic." Health Communication 36 (12): 1665–1673. https://doi.org/10.1080/10410236.2020.1847447.

"You can't calm the storm. So stop trying. What you can do is calm yourself. The storm will pass."
— Timber Hawkeye[15]

Doomscrolling isn't a sign you're broken. It's a sign you're looking for control in the only place you've been taught to look. But your power lives in what you do, not what you read.

THE DOPAMINE EQUATION

Let's talk chemistry—briefly, I promise.

Dopamine is often misunderstood as the "pleasure" chemical. It's not. It's the anticipation chemical. It's what makes you check your phone. And check again. And again. Each time, your brain releases a little squirt of dopamine, whispering, "Maybe this time…" It's not the content that hooks us. It's the hope. But here's the twist: when you engage in meaningful action—exercise, community, creativity—your brain also releases dopamine. And that version comes with long-term emotional regulation. The difference? One type burns out your reward system. The other builds it. So no, you don't need to quit technology. You just need to reintroduce **intentionality**. If you want to scroll, scroll something joyful. Beautiful. Thought-provoking. If you want to consume, choose things that nourish. If you want to disengage, replace scrolling with connection, not just absence. You're not fighting your phone. You're retraining your instincts.

MICRO-DETOXES FOR YOUR BRAIN

This is where we get practical. You don't need a seven-day

---

15 Hawkeye, Timber. Buddhist Boot Camp. San Francisco: HarperOne, 2013.

silent retreat or a dramatic flip phone purchase to reset your dopamine system. Small steps work.

Try this:

» Leave your phone in another room while you sleep. Your brain needs a night shift, not a notification shift.

» Replace one scroll session with a five-minute walk. Physical motion disrupts mental loops.

» Practice the "one-tab rule"—no more than one news app open at a time.

» Schedule intentional "doom time." Yes, literally set a timer and allow 15 minutes of news updates, then stop. The structure reduces compulsivity.

These tiny acts teach your nervous system the radical idea that it can survive boredom, uncertainty, and silence. And in that silence, you often find the clarity you were searching for in the scroll.

FOR THE PARENTS: DIGITAL MIRRORS

This part is uncomfortable.

Kids don't do what we say. They do what we model. If you're buried in your phone during dinner, doomscrolling headlines while preaching presence, your child learns that fear is normal and connection is optional.

The American Academy of Pediatrics recommends the following:

» No screen time under two (except video chat)

» One hour max per day for kids 2–5, with co-viewing

» Tech-free zones like bedrooms and dining areas

But beyond these guidelines, what matters most is emotional modeling. Show your child what it looks like to choose joy. To walk away from fearmongering. To say, "That's enough for today," and mean it. Your nervous system teaches theirs. And your relationship with your phone becomes the template for theirs. No pressure. Okay, a little pressure. But you're not alone in this. You're part of a very large club of humans trying to parent during the apocalypse. The goal isn't perfection. It's repair. Show them that disconnection is survivable—and reconnection is always an option.

AND IF THE NEWS IS BAD?

Let's not kid ourselves. Sometimes, the headlines are real. Sometimes, the threats are tangible. Sometimes, things are falling apart. In those moments, remember that information is not the same as empowerment. Reading about a flood doesn't make you swim faster. Reading about injustice doesn't make you an activist. Reading about the collapse of the American attention span doesn't help unless you're willing to reclaim your own. So, what do you do? You map information to action. Every time you feel overwhelmed, ask, "What can I do in my actual life?" And if the answer is nothing, then walk away. Rest. Breathe. The world will still be spinning tomorrow. Let go of the illusion that consuming pain is noble. It's not. It's draining. And the people who need your help—your family, your community, yourself—need you to be present, not paralyzed.

THE LAST SCROLL

You will doomscroll again. That's not failure. That's design.

But now, you'll know what it is. You'll see the algorithm. You'll hear the whisper of your amygdala. And maybe—just maybe—you'll choose to close the app. You're not meant to live in crisis. You're built for resilience. Your ancestors survived plagues, famines, and empires. You can survive your own bedtime routine. So tonight, try this: Put the phone down. Take a breath. Notice the quiet. And remember that your sanity is not a luxury. It's a form of protest.

> *"It is not enough to be busy. So are the ants. The question is: What are we busy about?"*
>
> — Henry David Thoreau[16]

---

16 Thoreau, Henry David. A Week on the Concord and Merrimack Rivers. Boston: Ticknor and Fields, 1862

CHAPTER 5

From Coping to Margarita

_(When your self-care routine includes 3 Oz of Tequila
and a cry for help)_

Let's start with a toast. Not to success or balance or inner peace, but to survival. Because if you've made it this far into the book, chances are you've noticed that simply existing in the modern world feels a little like riding a mechanical bull during an earthquake while reading your layoff notice. And for many, survival comes with a twist of lime, a splash of denial, and a side of "just one more." Substance use—whether it's wine, weed, whiskey, or whatever the guy in HR gave you after that last Zoom meltdown—has become the unsung national pastime. It's not that people want to be drunk, numb, or zonked out. It's that we want relief, and we've been sold a very specific idea of what that relief should look like: cold, fizzy, maybe pink, and always available at the checkout line in a can that says "calm." We don't start drinking to become alcoholics. We drink to stop thinking. We pop edibles not for insight but to mute the chaos. And sometimes, the coping works. Until it doesn't.

NUMB NOW, REGRET LATER

Coping and numbing are cousins who show up to the same party wearing different outfits. One is trying to help you dance through the hard stuff; the other is just blocking the door to the fire escape. Most of us have trouble telling them apart—especially when we're tired, scared, and just trying to make it through Tuesday without a full existential spiral. In the age of automation and algorithmic rejection letters, numbing has become a default. Because what are you supposed to do when your industry vanishes, your value gets benchmarked against a chatbot, and your long-term financial strategy hinges on whether or not your startup still exists by Friday?

You pour a drink.

You light something.

You escape.

And here's the trap: those things work. At least, at first. They soothe. They relax. They create the illusion of control—just enough to get you through the moment. But the moment always returns. And the solution slowly becomes the problem.

> *"The chains of habit are too weak to be felt until they are too strong to be broken."*
>
> — **Samuel Johnson**[17]

17 Johnson, Samuel. The Life of Samuel Johnson. By James Boswell. London: Henry Baldwin, 1791.

THE CLINICAL CALM OF COLLAPSE

I've treated thousands of patients struggling with addiction. Alcohol. Opiates. Meth. Benzos. You name it. It's my specialty. My experience means this chapter isn't just theoretical; it's personal and professional. I've seen what this stuff does to good people trying to survive bad systems. From a psychiatric perspective, substances are a kind of DIY neurochemical override—a blunt-force hack on the human operating system. Alcohol, cannabis, opioids, and benzos all manipulate neurotransmitters like GABA and dopamine, tricking your brain into thinking it's safe. They offer a short-term ceasefire in the war zone of your nervous system. But peace bought on credit has interest. Your brain adapts. It builds tolerance. And then the baseline shifts. The dose that once helped you sleep now just makes you irritable and foggy. The wine that used to be "mom juice" becomes "Why did I say that on a work call?" The edible that once took the edge off now dissolves your memory of entire conversations. This isn't about character. This is about chemistry.

Addiction isn't moral failure. It's repetition wired into biology. The more your brain pairs "stress" with "substance," the more it skips straight to the fix without checking in with the rest of you.

ROBOTS, STRESS, AND THE RISE OF NUMB

Let's loop this back to AI Induced Stress Syndrome (AISS) and remember the Cliff Notes version—it is characterized by chronic anxiety, burnout, and loss of identity that arise when rapid technological advancement outpaces our ability to emotionally and psychologically adapt. Substances don't exist in a vacuum. They exist in context—and this context is collapsing in on itself like a dying star. People aren't drinking because they're broken. They're drinking because their jobs are gone, their news feeds are a disaster, their attention spans have been hijacked, and their self-worth has been algorithmically downvoted by their productivity app. Substances have become the duct tape on a leaky psychological dam. The modern workplace is a neuropsychiatric hazard zone. We've replaced pensions with hustle culture. We've turned "grinding" into an aesthetic. And we've normalized a level of digital overstimulation that would have made the average 1980s stockbroker cry in a phone booth. Now throw AI into that cocktail. It promises limitless productivity and simultaneously whispers, "You're replaceable." That's a special kind of existential dread—a dread people try to mute with microdoses and margaritas.

THE REBRANDING OF ADDICTION

We don't call it addiction anymore. We call it *self-care*. Wine is marketed as empowerment. Edibles come in pastel tins with handwritten fonts. Psilocybin is the new productivity hack. OxyContin, in its day, was advertised as non-addictive and doctor-recommended. Even the language has evolved to accommodate denial:

> » "Mommy juice"
> » "Self-medication"
> » "Unwinding"
> » "Just vibing"

But if you have to vibe yourself unconscious to survive a Tuesday, we need to talk.

"We're all just one bad week away from a coping mechanism becoming a dependency."
— Clinical note, unattributed
but accurate

A QUIET EPIDEMIC

Addiction rarely starts with a bang. It starts with a whisper and a wink. It hides in plain sight—inside respectable homes, tasteful barware, artisanal dispensaries, and health and wellness retreats where the tea is dosed and the yoga is monetized. There's no dramatic rock bottom. There's just slow erosion:

- » You laugh less
- » You sleep poorly
- » You lie to people you love
- » You skip the gym
- » You work hungover
- » You start building your calendar around the next high

And it doesn't look like a collapse. It looks like "high-functioning."

Until it doesn't.

AISS AND THE INEFFECTIVE SELF-MEDICATION TRAP

AISS symptoms—overwhelm, panic, attention fragmentation, sleep disruption, learned helplessness—are not solved by substances. They're *camouflaged*. Every time you sip, smoke, swallow, or snort your way through these symptoms, you're numbing the signal. But the signal still exists. It just starts screaming louder the next morning. Anxiety is not cured by cocktails. Burnout doesn't disappear after two gummies and a night of TikTok. These are complex, layered, systemic problems—and treating them with vodka is like putting a Band-Aid on a leaking dam. Except the Band-Aid is flammable.

CHOOSE YOUR HARD: RELAPSE EDITION

Let's bring back one of our most useful refrains:

Choose your hard.

It's hard to face your feelings.

It's hard to run from them.

It's hard to break the habit.

It's hard to need it every day.

It's hard to stay sober when you're anxious, broke, and overstimulated.

It's hard to rebuild your life around a dependency.

You get to choose your hard.

And some hards lead to healing. Others lead to regret. Coping through discomfort builds strength. Coping through sedation builds walls. One is a future. The other is a trap.

RESILIENCE STARTS WITH HONESTY

You don't need to join a monastery and switch to spirulina smoothies. But you do need to ask yourself one powerful question: "Is this helping me become the person I want to be?"

Not:

» "Is this legal?"

» "Is this normal?"

» "Is this microdosed?"

But does this move me toward the life I want to live?

Because if the answer is no, that's not shame. That's data. And data is what recovery is built on.

THE LONG GAME OF COMING BACK

Here's the good news: neuroplasticity is real. Your brain can recover. Your habits can shift. But not while you're still pouring wine on your prefrontal cortex every night like it's fertilizer for creativity. Recovery isn't some magical ninety-day montage where you run stairs and reconnect with your inner child. It's boring, repetitive, awkward work—but it's also effective. Start small:

> » Pause before the pour.
> » Ask yourself, "What am I actually feeling right now?"
> » Replace the ritual—not the reward.

Instead of pouring a drink, make a pot of tea. Instead of lighting a bowl, light a candle and cry in the bath. You don't need to become a monk. But maybe try drinking tea like one—slowly, with intention, while reminding yourself that you're actively not destroying your liver in the name of "winding down."

Real coping rarely makes the highlight reel. It's not glamorous. It's not branded. It doesn't arrive in sleek four-packs or promise transcendence in twelve ounces or less. In fact, most of the time, real coping is boring. It's awkward. It's the psychological equivalent of eating vegetables—you know it's good for you, but it rarely feels good in the moment. It looks like this: You sit down and journal even though your brain would rather scroll. You go for a walk when your body feels like cement. You eat something that didn't come in cellophane. You cry, not because it's cathartic or beautiful, but because your chest is tight and your options are limited. You text a friend and actually say how you're doing. You put your phone down and choose sleep over spiraling. And it doesn't fix everything. But something shifts. Because real coping doesn't erase the storm. It just teaches you how to stand in it without capsizing.

> *"Feelings are much like waves: we can't stop them from coming, but we can choose which ones to surf."*
> — Jonatan Mårtensson[18]

CONNECTION IS THE ANTIDOTE

If substances isolate us, connection is what stitches us back together. In my years treating addiction, I've seen this truth over and over again: People don't recover in shame. They recover in community. They recover when someone picks up the phone. When someone listens without fixing. When someone stays even when it's hard. You don't have to have all the answers. You don't even need a plan. You just need a lifeline. Call a friend. Call a therapist. Hell, call your future self and leave a voicemail that says, "I'm trying." Because that counts. That's where the healing begins—not with perfection, but with presence. And if the only words you can find are, "I don't want to do this anymore," then say them out loud. That's enough. That's a start. And sometimes, that's the lifeline someone else needs to hear, too.

____

18 Mårtensson, Jonatan. Quoted in Chicken Soup for the Soul: Think Positive. Edited by Jack Canfield, Mark Victor Hansen, and Amy Newmark. Cos Cob, CT: Chicken Soup for the Soul Publishing, 2010.

FINAL SIP

Let's be clear: You don't have to be perfect to heal. You just have to show up. You're not a failure because you're struggling. You're not broken because you've self-medicated. You're not weak because your coping mechanisms got out of hand. You're human and living in a time that punishes feeling and monetizes avoidance. But escape doesn't build resilience; it delays it. And every time you numb the ache instead of naming it, you're reinforcing the myth that you can't handle your own life. But you can. Not all at once. Not flawlessly. But in moments. So tonight, when the ache returns—and it will—try this instead: Notice it. Honor it. Name it. Then choose one small act that reminds you you're still here. Still capable. Still in charge of the next five minutes. Because even if the system is broken ... even if the robots are winning ... even if the margarita is calling your name in cursive script across a salt-rimmed glass—you still get to choose.

You choose the comeback.

You choose your hard.

And that, my friend, is where everything starts to shift.

CHAPTER 6

Children of the Disruption

How to raise kids who don't freak out when the
Wi-Fi goes down

LET'S TAKE A MOMENT TO APPRECIATE THE TERRIFYING miracle of parenting in the AI era. You're raising kids who may never learn to drive, who can summon ChatGPT to do their homework, who will likely interview with a robot someday, and who believe that watching someone else play Minecraft on YouTube is a legitimate hobby. It's tempting to panic. But here's the good news: Children are sponges. And the better news? You are the bucket they soak in. What you model—not what you say—is what sticks. If you want your kids to survive this swirling mess of automation, uncertainty, and digital dopamine, you don't need a PhD in machine learning. You need to be resilient in front of them. Because more than ever, our job isn't to prepare the path for the child. It's to prepare the child for the path—even if that path now includes AI tutors, deepfake threats, and social media algorithms that know their insecurities better than they do.

WELCOME TO THE GLITCHY FUTURE

The world your children are growing into is not the one you were raised in. You grew up blowing on Nintendo cartridges. They're growing up asking Alexa to solve math equations. You waited days to rent a VHS. They're swiping left on entertainment with the attention span of a caffeinated squirrel. And it's not just tech. It's the pace of change. Your grandparents lived through one or two major societal shifts. Your kids will experience dozens. Industries will vanish before they graduate high school. New jobs—Prompt Engineer, Metaverse Architect, Algorithm Therapist (yes, really)—will emerge faster than college can adapt. The American Academy of Pediatrics currently recommends no more than one hour of high-quality screen time per day for children aged 2–5. That's adorable. It's also as enforceable as a toddler naptime treaty during a thunderstorm. Realistically, your kid is being shaped by screens—and what they see, feel, and imitate while on them. So, how do you raise emotionally grounded kids when the ground itself is on fire and the sky is flickering with push notifications? You start by being honest. Not cynical. Not panicked. Honest.

MODEL WHAT YOU WANT THEM TO MIRROR

If there's one immutable law of parenting, it's that your kids are always watching. They see how you react when you lose a job. They watch you scroll through the news at 11 p.m. with your jaw clenched. They hear the sighs. They feel the dread.

And they copy it. This means your resilience isn't just your own personal survival skill. It's an inherited behavior. When you regulate your emotions in front of your kids, you're literally wiring their brains for stability. Do you practice mindfulness? They notice. Do you curse at the printer like it's a demon? They notice that too. Children don't need perfection. They need process. It's okay to say, "I'm overwhelmed today, so I'm going to go outside for a walk to clear my head." That's not weakness. That's a masterclass in self-regulation.

CURIOSITY: THE ANTIDOTE TO FEAR

One of the most protective traits in this new world is curiosity. Fear shuts down possibilities. Curiosity opens them back up. AI will make many things obsolete ... but not wonder. Not exploration. Not the hunger to understand. When your child asks you how robots work, don't say, "I don't know," and hand them an iPad. Say, "Let's find out together." Normalize not knowing. Normalize learning. Normalize growth. Teach them to question—not authority for its own sake, but systems, narratives, and habits. When TikTok tells them they need to look a certain way or hustle 24/7, help them ask why. Who benefits? What's the message beneath the message? This is how digital natives become digitally wise.

> *"Don't prepare the road for the child. Prepare the child for the road."*
>
> —Old parenting proverb, made
> terrifyingly relevant.

EMOTIONAL LITERACY IS THE NEW IQ

Let's be blunt: it's not enough for kids to be smart. They need to be emotionally literate—able to name their feelings, tolerate discomfort, and bounce back from disappointment without a prescription or a meme. Teach your kids that emotions aren't enemies. Sadness is a signal. Anger is information. Anxiety is a message, not a moral failing. This doesn't mean turning your living room into a therapy office. But it does mean ditching the old "stop crying or I'll give you something to cry about" nonsense. Instead, try, "I see you're frustrated. That makes sense. Let's figure it out together." Small language shifts. Big outcomes.

BOUNDARIES IN THE AGE OF THE INFINITE SCROLL

Here's the hardest truth: tech companies are better at manipulating your child's brain than you are at protecting it. That's not a failure. That's neuroscience vs. capitalism. Your job isn't to be perfect. It's to set boundaries and be consistent. Limit screen time not because you're a technophobe, but because your child's prefrontal cortex isn't fully developed, and Fortnite is designed to bypass it. Encourage boredom. That's where creativity is born. Resist the urge to outsource parenting to screens. Yes, it's hard. Yes, it's easier to hand them a tablet than have a meltdown in the grocery store. But remember that what's easier in the moment is often harder in the long run. Also, for the record, it's okay to fail at this sometimes. You're not a robot. You're a human raising other humans—in a world increasingly designed for machines.

At the time of writing this book, my wife and I are deep

in the trenches with two tiny humans: a wild, joyful, seventeen-month-old boy who approaches life like a contact sport, and a brilliant, equally wild, three-and-a-half-year-old daughter who could probably out-negotiate most UN ambassadors. We decided early on—no TVs in the house. None. Zero. It's one of those convictions we hold with the kind of intensity usually reserved for CrossFitters and sourdough bakers. And yet—full transparency—once a month, I travel overnight for work. And on those nights, guess who tucks the kids in? Blippi, the popular orange bow tie wearing kids show character. In all his high-pitched, suspender-clad chaos. Because as much as we believe in boundaries, we also believe in sanity. Sometimes, choosing your hard means sticking to your principles. Other times, it means handing the remote to your exhausted partner and saying, "Let the man in orange handle it tonight."

DISRUPTION AS OPPORTUNITY

The same forces that are destabilizing the world are also creating space for transformation. Automation will remove jobs, yes. But it will also remove drudgery. AI might disrupt the classroom. But it also might individualize learning in ways never before possible. Help your kids see disruption not just as loss, but as a reframe. Teach them to ask, "What's opening up here? What new skills can I develop? How do I stay adaptable?" Resilience is about learning to bend without breaking and teaching your kids that bending is beautiful.

EVIDENCE-BASED RESILIENCE: RAISING STRONGER HUMANS (WITHOUT ENROLLING THEM IN A NINJA ACADEMY)

It's not all gut instinct, bribery, and the occasional primal scream into a dish towel. We actually have research-backed tools that help children become more emotionally agile, mentally tough, and slightly less likely to live in your basement at age 35.

1. Problem-Solving Skills

Children who are guided—not steamrolled—through their struggles tend to develop higher resilience, according to studies in developmental psychology. In plain terms: stop fixing everything. The next time your child melts down because their LEGO tower collapsed for the third time, don't grab the glue gun. Instead, say something wildly therapeutic like, "What could we try next?" Yes, they might sob and throw a brick at the cat, but you've just activated their prefrontal cortex. Well done, Coach Cortex.

Example: Your kid can't find their shoes. Instead of turning into a one-person SEAL Team Six, ask, "Where's the last place your shoes remember being?" It's annoying. It's slow. And it works. Eventually.

2. Growth Mindset Language

Carol Dweck's research gave us the magical power of "yet." Instead of "I can't do math," it becomes "I can't do math yet." One is a dead end. The other is a detour with snacks.

Example: Your kid draws a potato with legs and calls it a horse. They cry because it doesn't look like the horse on their iPad. Don't say, "Well, not everyone's an artist." Say, "You're still learning. Want to try drawing the legs from a photo?" Then get ready for ten more potato horses. Progress.

3. Gratitude Practices

Gratitude journaling isn't just for Instagram therapists. It rewires the brain. Kids who learn to notice the good—even a tiny bit of good—are better at bouncing back from disappointment.

Example: Your child just got told they can't have a second popsicle. Tears. Rage. Existential despair. Once they've cooled off, ask: "What was one fun thing we did today?" Boom. Gratitude grenade. Bonus if you model it by saying something like, "I'm grateful we didn't burn down the kitchen trying to make slime."

4. Self-Regulation Training

Regulation is the new superpower. Breathing techniques, progressive muscle relaxation, and even five-second body scans can calm a child's nervous system faster than a juice box. Tools like *Headspace for Kids* or *Smiling Mind* actually work—and don't require a PhD to use.

Example: Your child is losing their mind because their sibling touched their dinosaur. Instead of joining them in the emotional Hunger Games, say: "Let's do dragon breaths—breathe in like you're about to roar, and out like you're blowing fire." Is it ridiculous? Yes. Does it work? Also, yes.

5. Meaningful Chores

Turns out, giving kids chores doesn't ruin childhood. It wires their brains for capability. The Harvard Grant Study (which followed people for 75+ years) found that doing age-appropriate chores is linked to stronger adult relationships and a sense of purpose.

Example: Your four-year-old spills cereal. You could clean it. Or you could hand them a mini broom and say, "You're on the cleanup crew today." It may take ten times longer, but it will make them feel like a capable part of the team. Welcome to the resistance.

6. Autonomy-Supportive Parenting

This one's simple but brutal: Let them fail. Let them choose. Support, don't rescue. Autonomy isn't about being hands-off; it's about saying, "I believe in your ability to try this and learn something—even if you fall on your butt."

Example: Your kid wants to wear pajamas to school. Let them. (Unless there's a dress code, in which case, let them wear the weird outfit with socks over their pants.) Natural consequences teach faster than lectures. And remember, you can still take a photo for blackmail later.

These aren't magic tricks. They're scaffolding for the messy, magnificent process of becoming human. And yes, they take time. But so does therapy—and this is way cheaper. This isn't woo-woo. It's strategy. Raising emotionally intelligent, adaptive children isn't a mystery; it's a methodology.

YOU ARE THE BLUEPRINT

More than rules, more than advice, your presence is what matters. If you want kids who can adapt, you need to show them how to adapt. If you want kids who can regulate, show them what regulation looks like—not just when things are good, but especially when they aren't. Cry in front of them. Apologize when you lose it. Celebrate small wins. Laugh when things go sideways. Let them see the mess. Let them see the repair. You don't need to be a flawless robot-parent. You just need to be real.

> *"The way we talk to our children becomes their inner voice."*
>
> — Peggy O'Mara[19]

CHOOSE YOUR HARD—TOGETHER

Hard things don't go away. They evolve. So do you. So do your kids. Teach them early that it's hard to stay present in a chaotic world. But it's also hard to live disconnected from your own values. It's hard to practice empathy when the world feels transactional. But it's harder to be raised by robots. It's hard to parent in a collapsing system. But it's harder to unteach survival mode. Choose your hard. And let your kids see you do it. Because if there's one thing more powerful than a child growing up in a world of disruption, it's a child growing up in a home that models what it means to face that disruption with heart, humor, and hope.

When my wife and I decided to have children, we came up with a family motto—a sort of evolving manifesto forged in the fires of sleep deprivation and crushed Goldfish crackers. We've edited it over time, trimmed the fluff, and laughed at what stuck. Eventually, we boiled it down to the essentials:

---

19 O'Mara, Peggy. Peggy O'Mara's Natural Family Living: The Mothering Magazine Guide to Parenting. New York: Atria Books, 2000.

Alfanos are kind.

Alfanos can do hard things.

Alfanos have grit.

And—perhaps most importantly—Alfanos don't eat cats.

That last one was added by our daughter when she was two, and for reasons we may never fully understand, it's remained enshrined in the family code. And honestly? It tracks. You never know when you're raising the next great humanitarian or a low-key supervillain.

And, here's the thing—I genuinely believe that crafting a family motto might be one of the most sneakily genius things a parent can do. It's low effort, high yield. Like crockpot parenting. Because your kids are not going to remember what they got for their fifth birthday. They won't recall the emotionally fraught negotiations over ice cream or that time they turned into human gravel after wiping out on their bike. But they *will* remember the stuff you chant like a cult leader before school drop-off. If you model it, repeat it, and brand it like it's your family's emotional startup, it sticks. Eventually, it becomes less of a motto and more of a neural firmware update.

Congratulations, you've just installed Kindness v3.2 and Anti-Cat-Eating Protocol.

A FINAL WORD (BEFORE THEY ASK CHATGPT INSTEAD)

Your kids are growing up in a world where information is infinite, attention is currency, and emotional resilience is a superpower. They don't need you to be perfect. They need you to be steady. This book isn't just for you. It's for them, because everything you do to stabilize yourself, to learn how to outrun dread, and to reclaim your mind from the robots is part of their inheritance. Let them watch you evolve. Let them see you adapt. Because in the end, that's how we build a generation that won't just survive disruption, but will lead through it.

> *"The greatest gift you can give your children is your own emotional healing."*
>
> — Anonymous, but wise

CHAPTER 7

Cognitive Behavioral Therapy (CBT)

Tools That Actually Work

Or How to Gaslight Your Brain in a Therapeutic Way

Let's face it—when the world is falling apart, the last thing you want to hear is that your salvation lies in journaling. Or that your brain, that traitorous meatball whispering doom in your ear, can somehow be tricked into behaving with something called a "thought log." But here we are. Cognitive Behavioral Therapy (CBT) is the mental health equivalent of a daily vitamin. Not trendy. Not sexy. But effective. Boringly, statistically, almost annoyingly effective.

The idea is deceptively simple: Your thoughts, emotions, and behaviors are a tangled trio doing an awkward conga line through your life. Change one, and you can shift the rhythm of the whole dance. CBT doesn't care how deeply your trauma runs or how many past lives your anxiety has had. It asks one question: What are you thinking right now, and is it helping? Because the reality is that resilience doesn't come from having the perfect childhood or never experiencing hardship. It comes from developing tools—repeatable, concrete, science-backed tools—to confront your own mind when it starts spinning stories about how everything is doomed, and you are too.

THIS IS YOUR BRAIN ON PANIC

Let's take a walk through a typical cognitive spiral. It starts with a trigger. Maybe you get a Slack notification at 9:01 a.m. that says, "Can we talk?" Maybe your checking account dips below $100. Maybe you read a headline that says, "AI to Replace 90% of Jobs by 2026." You think, *Great. I'll just go eat bark and live in the woods.* Immediately, your brain fills in the blanks—catastrophically. It's an evolutionary leftover from our ancient ancestors: whoever panicked first lived longer than the ones who stopped to wonder if the dire wolf looked friendly. But your brain doesn't know the difference between a wolf and a calendar invite. Instead, it reacts like the world is ending. Your heart races. Your muscles tense. Your attention narrows to all the possible disasters ahead.

This is where CBT steps in—not with a hug, but with a clipboard.

CBT therapists aren't interested in rubbing your back while you spiral. They want to know what that spiral is made of, in which direction it's spinning, and how often you ride it like a sad carousel. They're like emotional meteorologists with a specialty in calling out brain fog.

DECATASTROPHIZING: THE ART OF TALKING YOURSELF OFF THE LEDGE

CBT's greatest party trick is "decatastrophizing," which is just a fancy term for reality-checking your own panic. It's like an investigation. Let's say you get that "Can we talk?" message from your boss. Your brain immediately thinks, "I'm being fired. I'll lose my health insurance. I'll never work again. I'll end up living in my car, eating discount crackers." Decatastrophizing says, "Hold on. What's the actual evidence?"

> » Has your boss said anything negative recently?
> » Could "Can we talk?" mean literally anything else?
> » Have you catastrophized before and been wrong?

Now ask, "What's the most likely outcome?" Often, the answer is a boring conversation about workflow, not a corporate firing squad. This tool isn't magic, but it interrupts the spiral long enough for you to get your footing. It creates space between reaction and reality. And that's where resilience lives.

> *"Anxiety is a false prophet. It tells you the worst-case scenario as if it's gospel."*
>
> — **Every CBT Therapist Ever**

Another variation of this practice includes imagining a third party—someone neutral, perhaps even your slightly judgmental aunt—listening to your internal monologue and fact-checking it. Would she raise an eyebrow and ask, "Really, Steve? You think a typo in the email means you're about to get axed?" If so, it's a clue that you've entered the doom spiral. And don't underestimate the power of speaking your catastrophic thought out loud. Say it to a friend, or a dog, or a plant—and listen to how absurd it sounds. "I think if I mess up this spreadsheet, the IRS will take my house, and my cat will never love me again." Suddenly, it doesn't carry quite the same weight.

THOUGHT TRACKING: BECOME A DETECTIVE IN YOUR OWN MIND

If you've ever kept a food journal to track calories, you already know the premise of thought tracking: you can't change what you don't observe. CBT uses "thought logs" to help you catch distorted thinking in the wild. Because your thoughts don't announce themselves as lies. They feel true. That's what makes them dangerous. A thought log looks like this:

> » **Trigger:** I saw a news article about layoffs.
> » **Automatic Thought:** I'm next. I won't be able to support my family.
> » **Emotion:** Panic, helplessness, shame
> » **Cognitive Distortion:** Fortune-telling, catastrophizing, all-or-nothing thinking
> » **Rational Response:** I have no evidence that I'm being laid off. Even if I were, I have options and support.
> » **New Emotion:** Concern, but grounded

Yes, it's tedious. Yes, it feels weird at first. But repetition is how your brain learns. The more you challenge distortions, the more automatic the rational voice becomes. A 2020 study in *Behavior Research and Therapy* showed that consistent thought tracking reduced generalized anxiety symptoms by nearly 40% over twelve weeks.[20] Not with meds. Not with mushrooms. With awareness.

Pro tip: If writing isn't your thing, use your phone. Voice memos. Notes app. Sharpie on a napkin. The format doesn't matter; the habit does. Over time, you start to see patterns. Maybe your anxiety spikes after family dinners or doom-scrolling Twitter. Now you've got data. And data is power. It's emotional cartography—you're mapping the terrain of your own nervous system.

BEHAVIORAL ACTIVATION: ACTION FIRST, MOOD SECOND

Here's a CBT truth bomb: waiting to feel motivated is a trap. Behavioral activation flips the script. Instead of waiting to feel better before you act, you act your way into feeling better. Think of it this way: depression and anxiety are emotional inertia. They tell you to stop, withdraw, and avoid. The brain mistakes inactivity for safety. But inactivity becomes the problem.

CBT says to start small. Move your body. Make a call. Wash a dish. Go outside for five minutes. This isn't "positive vibes only" nonsense. It's an evidence-based intervention. You act → you feel accomplished → your mood shifts → your brain learns. And yes, on some days, it will still feel like dragging yourself through wet cement. That's okay. Choose your hard. It's hard to feel depressed. It's also hard to go for a walk when you're anxious. But only one of those hards

---

20 Najmi, Sadia, and Richard G. Heimberg. 2020. "Effects of Thought Monitoring and Cognitive Restructuring on Symptoms of Generalized Anxiety Disorder." Behaviour Research and Therapy 132: 103654. https://doi.org/10.1016/j.brat.2020.103654.

moves you forward.

Want another underutilized strategy? Schedule your day like your own overbearing boss. Block out time for a walk, a chore, even ten minutes of staring at a tree. When your brain is a chaotic mess of intrusive thoughts, structure is a kindness. And when in doubt, do something small, then celebrate the living hell out of it. "I took a shower today" can be a triumph.

COGNITIVE DISTORTIONS: YOUR BRAIN'S GREATEST HITS

CBT teaches you to spot recurring thought errors:

» **All-or-Nothing Thinking:** "If I fail this, I'm a total failure."

» **Mind Reading:** "They're mad at me. I just know it."

» **Should Statements:** "I should be further along by now."

» **Personalization:** "It's my fault the meeting went badly."

The goal isn't to stop having distorted thoughts. You're human. The goal is to spot them and respond differently. You are not your thoughts. You're the observer of them. And observers can intervene. Imagine giving each distortion a character. The Should Have Monster. The Catastrophe Clown. The Mind Reader Mime. Name them. Draw them. When they show up, say, "Oh, hey, it's the Drama Llama again. What are you shouting about today?" Humor disarms the distortion. Naming separates you from it. You get to choose how much power it holds.

REAL TOOLS, REAL STAKES

CBT isn't just for the worried well. These tools are used in:

- » PTSD recovery
- » Substance abuse programs
- » Chronic pain management
- » Postpartum anxiety treatment

And for good reason. They're adaptable, skill-based, and empirically supported. In the era of AI-induced stress syndrome, we need more than vague advice and mindfulness memes. We need tools that fit into everyday life—the lives of people balancing Zoom meetings, economic instability, and intrusive thoughts that whisper, "You're not doing enough." CBT doesn't ask you to be fearless. It asks you to respond to fear with skill. It works for the ICU nurse with twelve-hour shifts. For the teenager trying to exist without a filter. For the single parent doing bedtime and spreadsheets simultaneously. You don't need to be a Zen monk. You need three minutes of clarity and a pen.

AISS isn't some abstract techie affliction; it's a clinically relevant state defined by five hallmark symptoms: chronic hypervigilance, digital doomscrolling, identity disruption, emotional dysregulation, and cognitive overload. Fortunately, CBT is the antidote.

Hypervigilance? Decatastrophizing slows the alarm bells and asks for evidence. Doomscrolling? Thought tracking interrupts the mental junk food and replaces it with mindful observation. Identity disruption? Cognitive reframing restores a sense of agency and coherence. Emotional dysregulation? Self-regulation tools and behavioral activation stabilize the nervous system. Cognitive overload? CBT offers structure, pacing, and prioritization.

In a world where algorithms are optimized for anxiety, CBT is optimized for clarity. It doesn't fight the chaos with more noise. It brings a map, a toolkit, and the audacity to say, "You don't have to believe every thought your brain throws at you."

PRACTICE OVER PERFECTION

If CBT were a person, it would gently say, "You don't have to do this perfectly. You just have to notice." It's okay if you forget to write things down. It's okay if your thought log looks like a mess. The point is engagement. The act of showing up to your own mind is a radical choice in a world that wants you to numb out. Resilience doesn't come from being unshakable. It comes from practicing balance after the fall. You're not weak for needing structure. You're smart for building it. Start where you are. Track one thought. Challenge one belief. Move your body once. Repeat. It doesn't need to be revolutionary to be effective.

> *"You can't stop the waves, but you can learn to surf."*
> — Jon Kabat-Zinn[21]

---

21 Kabat-Zinn, Jon. *Wherever You Go, There You Are: Mindfulness Meditation in Everyday Life.* New York: Hyperion, 1994.

CHAPTER 8

Still Mode, Activated

---

*Or Meditation for People Who Don't Own a
Singing Bowl*

LET'S BE HONEST, THE WORD "MINDFULNESS" HAS suffered a slow and painful PR death. It's been printed on too many throw pillows, tattooed on too many yoga instructors, and shoved into too many corporate slide decks next to words like synergy and optimization. For most of us, the idea of sitting quietly and breathing feels about as useful as rearranging deck chairs on a sinking cruise ship. Especially when your mind is full of flashing headlines, half-read emails, and that one unshakable worry that AI is going to steal your job and your personality. But mindfulness, when stripped of its robes and incense, is not some mystical cure-all. It's a neurological tool. A performance upgrade. And for a brain fried by overstimulation and existential dread, it's one of the only things that actually helps you stop panicking and start responding.

Welcome to Still Mode.

YOU'RE NOT BROKEN—YOU'RE OVERSTIMULATED

Your brain is not malfunctioning. It's doing exactly what it was built to do—scan for threats, analyze problems, keep you alive. But in 2025, the "threats" aren't actually threatening. They're notifications. Algorithms. Layoff rumors. The neighbor's ring camera that caught you walking out to check the mail in your bathrobe again. Modern life is relentlessly activating. Your nervous system was designed for bursts of danger, followed by long stretches of calm. Instead, you're living in a world that's flipped the ratio: hours of low-grade panic, punctuated by random doom-scrolling and iced coffee. This is why stillness feels weird. It's not because it's unnatural. It's because your system has forgotten how to access it.

THE SCIENCE BEHIND STILL MODE

Mindfulness isn't just a spiritual practice. It's a neurological recalibration. When you engage in intentional stillness—whether through breath, observation, or focused attention—you activate your parasympathetic nervous system. That's the "rest and digest" setting. The opposite of fight-or-flight. Functional MRI scans show that regular mindfulness practice reduces activation in the amygdala (your fear center) and strengthens the prefrontal cortex (your executive function center). In short, you react less, think more, and become harder to emotionally hijack. It's not magic. It's math.

"You should sit in meditation for twenty minutes a day. Unless you're too busy. Then you should sit for an hour."
— **Zen Proverb (or your therapist, probably)**

A 2018 randomized, controlled trial published in *Psychiatry Research* found that participants who practiced mindfulness meditation for just eight weeks showed significantly lower levels of cortisol—the stress hormone—compared to the control group. Not only that, but their scores on measures of emotional resilience increased by more than 30%.

WHAT STILL MODE ACTUALLY LOOKS LIKE

Let's ditch the fantasy version. No mountaintop. No candles. No music made by wind chimes and whales. Here's what it really looks like:

» You sit down, stand, or lie flat on the floor
» You close your eyes (optional) and take a breath
» Your brain starts listing everything you forgot to do
» You notice that happening
» You come back to your breath, your feet, or the sound of the refrigerator
» You do this **over and over**, like a goldfish in therapy

That's it. That's the game.

Mindfulness is not a state of perfect Zen. It's a loop: lose focus → come back → lose focus → come back. Every return builds mental muscle. Every interruption is part of the practice.

FOR THE SKEPTICS: WHY IT'S NOT WOO

If you're someone who rolls their eyes at meditation apps and equates "being present" with wasting time, let's reframe it.

Mindfulness = Cognitive Control. You're learning to direct attention on purpose. That's power.

Stillness = Strategic Pause. You can't solve a problem when your brain is on fire. Still mode lets the flames die down so you can see clearly.

Focus = Efficiency. Mindfulness improves working memory, concentration, and even creativity. It's not about doing less. It's about doing smarter.

A 2022 systematic review in *Clinical Psychology Review* found that mindfulness-based interventions significantly reduced symptoms in anxiety, depression, and PTSD populations.[22] And the gains weren't just psychological—many subjects reported better sleep, improved digestion, and reduced physical pain.

TRAINING THE BRAIN TO RESPOND, NOT REACT

One of the most dangerous myths we tell ourselves is, "I can't help it. That's just how I am." Mindfulness says, "Actually, you can train for that." You can train to pause before snapping at your partner. You can train to notice the early signs of spiraling before you end up six tabs deep in Reddit and shame. You can take a moment to think, "Should I actually have this cocktail?" You can train to stay grounded when the world around you is spinning. This is the essence of emotional regulation. Not suppression. Not stoicism. Regulation. And it's one of the strongest predictors of long-term resilience.

---

22 Goldberg, Simon B., Ryan M. Riordan, Matthew J. Sun, and Richard J. Davidson. 2022. "The Efficacy of Mindfulness-Based Interventions for Mental Health: A Systematic Review and Meta-Analysis." Clinical Psychology Review 91: 102111. https://doi.org/10.1016/j.cpr.2021.102111.

"The greatest weapon against stress is our ability to choose one thought over another."
— William James[23]

Stillness creates that space.

THE HIDDEN COST OF NEVER STOPPING

If you're constantly moving, scrolling, refreshing, planning, reacting … ask yourself why. What are you avoiding? Most people aren't afraid of silence. They're afraid of what will rise up in it. Still Mode forces you to meet your mind without a buffer. And sometimes that means encountering the parts of yourself that are scared, grieving, ashamed, or just plain tired. But here's the paradox: when you allow those parts to exist, they start to quiet down. You stop being at war with your own internal landscape. Avoidance takes energy. Presence builds it.

STILL MODE IN DAILY LIFE (NO RETREAT REQUIRED)

You don't need a retreat or an app to do this. You just need a moment and a bit of intention.

Exercise 1: Stillness in traffic: Turn off the podcast. Breathe. Feel your hands on the wheel. Pick a sensory input and anchor to it. Notice the feeling of the seat beneath you, the hum of the engine, your breath in and out. When your thoughts drift to your inbox or to-do list, gently bring them back.

Exercise 2: Dishwashing Meditation: Feel the water. Notice the temperature. Smell the soap. Listen to the clink of

---

23 James, William. The Principles of Psychology. New York: Henry Holt and Company, 1890.

plates. Breathe. This is stillness in motion.

Exercise 3: Evening Scan: Before bed, lie down. Scan your body from head to toe. Don't judge the sensations. Just notice them. If your mind wanders to what you didn't finish today or what might happen tomorrow, smile and return to the sensation of breath in your belly.

Exercise 4: One-Minute Anchor: Set a timer for one minute. During that minute, pick one physical sensation (e.g., breath, heartbeat, feet on the floor) and return to it every time your mind drifts. You'll be amazed at what happens in sixty seconds of intentional attention.

Each moment is a doorway to presence. You just have to step through.

TEACHING STILL MODE TO THE NEXT GENERATION

If you're a parent, teacher, or mildly responsible adult, you have an even bigger reason to engage with this. Kids learn regulation by watching it. They mirror nervous systems. If you model anxiety, they absorb it. If you model stillness, they learn it's possible. You don't need to lecture them about mindfulness. Just practice pausing. Let them see you breathe instead of yelling. Let them watch you slow down instead of speeding up. In Chapter 6, we talked about modeling emotional resilience for children. Stillness is one of the most powerful ways to do that. And yes, they'll roll their eyes. Do it anyway.

YOU'RE NOT LAZY. YOU'RE HEALING.

One of the most radical things you can do in a hyper-productive, overstimulated culture is nothing. Not as avoidance.

But as a choice. Choosing stillness means saying, "I matter enough to rest. To listen. To exist without performing." It means remembering that you're a human being, not a human doing. And in a world where robots never need to pause, the ability to stop might just be our most human strength.

> *"Sometimes the most important thing in a whole day is the rest we take between two deep breaths."*
> — **Etty Hillesum**[24]

---

24 Hillesum, Etty. An Interrupted Life: The Diaries, 1941–1943, and Letters from Westerbork. New York: Henry Holt and Company, 1996.

CHAPTER 9

Outrun the Existential Dread

____

Or Cardio for When You Can't Outrun Your Feelings,
but You're Sure as Hell Going to Try

THERE'S SOMETHING ABSURDLY POETIC ABOUT jogging while having an existential crisis. There you are—lungs burning, thighs on fire, sweating through your old college hoodie—while your brain is softly whispering, "What's the point of anything?"

Welcome to modern exercise.

For many of us, movement has become less about six-pack abs and more about fending off collapse. It's not a fitness routine. It's a coping mechanism. And frankly, it's a damn good one. This chapter is not going to guilt you into joining CrossFit or convince you that burpees will save your soul. But it will make the case—scientifically, psychologically, and sarcastically—that physical movement is one of the most underrated weapons we have in the fight against dread, despair, and the ever-looming threat of robotic job theft. Because while you may not be able to bench press your way out of late-stage capitalism, you can rewire your brain with a brisk walk.

MOVEMENT AS MEDICINE: ANOTHER ANTIDOTE FOR AISS

AI Induced Stress Syndrome isn't a fictional diagnosis anymore. With hallmark symptoms like chronic hypervigilance, emotional dysregulation, and cognitive overload, AISS is our generation's burnout cocktail, shaken with a side of algorithmic dread. And while therapy, CBT, and medication are effective tools, exercise may be the missing physical pillar of treatment. Here's why: Physical activity directly counters each of the five core features of AISS.

Hypervigilance? Movement activates the parasympathetic nervous system, helping your brain exit the threat loop.

Doomscrolling? Exercise provides a competing behavioral response—one that reengages the body and disrupts compulsive mental habits.

Emotional dysregulation? The release of endorphins and serotonin supports mood stabilization.

Cognitive overload? Movement restores attention, simplifies neural pathways, and reduces the chaos inside your skull.

The science backs this up. A 2023 meta-analysis in *Nature Mental Health* found that even short bouts of moderate-intensity physical activity significantly reduced symptoms of anxiety and depression across all age groups.[25] Meanwhile, research from the Harvard School of Public Health shows that just fifteen minutes of running or an hour of walking per day reduces the risk of major depression by 26 percent.[26] In other words, exercise is your frontline defense against the digital apocalypse of the mind.

And here's the kicker: when compared head-to-head with medications like anti-depressants and anti-anxiolytics exercise performs just as well, if not better, in several populations. A 2018 study published in *JAMA Psychiatry* concluded that exercise interventions were as effective as pharmacologic treatments for adults with mild to moderate depression, without the side effects often associated with antidepressants.[27] In short, a brisk jog does not come with a black-box warning. The prescription? Movement, prescribed generously and without judgment. Side effects may include reduced despair, improved sleep, enhanced cognition, and a slightly elevated tolerance for LinkedIn posts about AI startups.

25 Rebar, Amanda L., Simon Rosenbaum, Felipe B. Schuch, and Joseph Firth. 2023. "Physical Activity and Mental Health: A Meta-Analysis of Dose–Response Effects Across Age Groups." Nature Mental Health 1 (3): 210–223. https://doi.org/10.1038/s44220-023-00045-9.

26 Harvard T.H. Chan School of Public Health. 2018. "Running or Walking May Reduce Risk of Depression." Harvard T.H. Chan School of Public Health News, November 1, 2018. https://www.hsph.harvard.edu/news/hsph-in-the-news/running-or-walking-may-reduce-risk-of-depression/.

27 Schuch, Felipe B., Davy Vancampfort, Brendon Stubbs, Joseph Firth, Simon Rosenbaum, and Andreas Rebar. 2018. "Exercise as a Treatment for Depression: A Systematic Review and Meta-Analysis of Randomized Clinical Trials." JAMA Psychiatry 75 (6): 545–554. https://doi.org/10.1001/jamapsychiatry.2018.1468.

THE EXISTENTIAL TREADMILL

Let's take a quick inventory of things weighing on the collective psyche: AI is coming for your job, the climate is doing whatever the opposite of chilling is, you're sleep-deprived, chronically online, and slowly becoming part of the couch. It's no wonder your body is screaming for movement. Not just to burn calories—but to process emotion. When we don't move, we stagnate. Not just physically, but mentally. Emotionally. Spiritually. We stew in our thoughts. We marinate in our helplessness. We scroll ourselves into paralysis. Movement cuts through the fog.

YOUR BRAIN ON EXERCISE: THE SCIENCE

Exercise is one of the most effective, fastest-acting antidepressants known to humanity. And no, that's not fitness cult propaganda, that's decades of data. Regular physical activity increases levels of brain-derived neurotrophic factor (BDNF), which helps neurons grow, survive, and repair. It's like fertilizer for your brain. Movement also floods your system with endorphins, dopamine, and serotonin—chemicals that literally make life feel more manageable.

> *"Exercise is the single most powerful tool you have to optimize your brain function."*
>
> — John Ratey, MD[28]

In randomized controlled trials, exercise performs on par with SSRIs for mild to moderate depression. It also improves executive function, reduces anxiety, enhances memory, and

---

28 Ratey, John J. Spark: The Revolutionary New Science of Exercise and the Brain. New York: Little, Brown and Company, 2008.

builds the kind of grit that makes you more resistant to stress. And it doesn't have to be intense. Even twenty minutes of walking can trigger a cascade of mood-lifting effects. Movement is medicine. It's just hard to sell because it doesn't come in a bottle.

MOVEMENT IS NOT A PERFORMANCE

Modern fitness culture wants you to believe that if your movement isn't logged, timed, tracked, or compared, it doesn't count. This is a lie created by wearable tech, Instagram, and that guy from high school who talks about "grind culture" on his lunch breaks. Real movement, the kind that nourishes your nervous system, doesn't need metrics. It needs presence. You can dance like a dying octopus, stretch like a distracted cat, or walk like you're late to a job you hate. All of it counts. There is no PR for healing. There is no gold star for coming back to yourself. You're not doing this for applause. You're doing it because your brain is on fire, and movement is the water.

EXERCISE AS MICRO-REBELLION: WHY IT WORKS WHEN NOTHING ELSE DOES

When everything feels beyond your control—the economy, your inbox, the fact that your favorite restaurant is now a vape store—movement reminds you that action is still possible. This is not just symbolic. It's neurochemical. Each step, stretch, or squat tells your brain, "We're not stuck." That shift matters. In psychology, behavioral activation is one of the foundational tools in treating depression. You act first. The mood follows. Waiting to feel motivated is like waiting for your smartphone to apologize—it's not going to happen. So, you start small. A lap around the kitchen island. Ten jumping jacks while waiting for your coffee to brew. Stretching your arms overhead like a confused toddler trying to make a point. It's not about burning calories. It's about building inertia.

STRETCHING THE TRUTH (GENTLY)

If cardio feels like a betrayal of your personality, there's good news: stretching counts. Gentle, mindful movements like yoga or even basic dynamic stretches can ground you just as effectively.

Need an example? Try the "I-hate-this-meeting" shoulder roll. Sit tall, inhale, lift your shoulders to your ears, exhale, drop them like you just gave up caring. Do it three times. You just did mindful movement.

Want another? Forward fold. Stand tall, exhale, and bend forward slowly, letting your arms hang. Bonus points if you whisper, "I am the chaos" as you reach for your toes. The point is not form. It's awareness. When you're in your body, you're not lost in your head.

THE RITUAL OF MOVEMENT

Ritual doesn't mean chanting in candlelight (unless that's your thing). It means repetition with meaning. Walking every evening with no headphones. Doing five pushups at the end of your workday to signal "this laptop is now dead to me." Shaking out your arms like you're trying to fling off all the emails you didn't answer. These tiny rituals re-anchor your day. They remind you that your body is not just a meat vehicle for your anxious brain.

MOVEMENT FOR THE HOPELESS DAYS

Not every day is a mountain. Some are swamps. On those days, the movement might be a single stretch in bed. A walk to the mailbox. A shaky squat while brushing your teeth. That still counts. The myth of "go hard or go home" has no place in a world full of burnout. Instead, we go gentle and stay out of the ER. Here's a mini routine for hopeless days:

1. Lie on your back. Bring knees to chest. Squeeze. Breathe.
2. Rock gently side to side. Imagine massaging your spine with your own dissatisfaction.
3. Roll to your side. Sit up slowly. Tell yourself, "I'm still in the game."

PARENTING IN MOTION

If you've got kids, movement is survival. But it's also modeling. When they see you stretch, breathe, and move through stress instead of snapping, they learn regulation. Make it silly. Make it noisy. Have a dance battle before homework. Do yoga poses with names you invent, like "angry jellyfish" or "slouchy giraffe." You're not just exercising. You're co-regulating. You're shaping how they'll move through their own storms.

YOU'RE NOT LAZY. YOU'RE TIRED.

Here's the final truth bomb: What you're calling laziness might be something else. Tired. Stuck. Overwhelmed. Burnt out. Movement isn't punishment for inactivity. It's medicine for disconnection. A reunion with yourself. And in a world that's trying to automate everything, moving your own damn limbs might be the most human act left.

CHAPTER 10

Upgrade Complete

Or How to Survive the Future Without Becoming a Cyborg or a Cynic

You made it.

If this were a video game, this is where your screen would flash: Achievement Unlocked—Mentally Stable (for now). Confetti would fall. A robot would hand you a participation trophy made of recycled iPhones. And you'd quietly wonder if the real prize was the dopamine we regulated along the way. But this isn't a game. This is life in the middle of the Fourth Industrial Revolution. And it doesn't come with a tutorial or a pause button. Still, here you are—ten chapters wiser, slightly more self-aware, and hopefully no longer Googling "how to survive AI without crying." This final chapter is your reminder that you're not broken—you're adapting. Let's make it official. You don't have to become a perfect, enlightened, kale-consuming cyborg to thrive in this world.

You just have to be slightly more prepared, a lot more con-nected, and capable of laughing while the algorithms eat your job and recommend cat memes at the same time. Let's keep going.

THE MYTH OF MASTERY

Let's burst a bubble right off the bat: no one ever finishes healing, adjusting, or figuring it all out. That's not how humans work. The idea that we can "complete" a mental health journey like finishing a Netflix series is comforting but false. Resilience is not a destination. It's a lifestyle. You don't meditate once, outrun your dread with a single jog, or cog-nitive-behavioral your way into eternal emotional stability. What you do is practice. You show up. You keep moving. You fall down, adapt, and reapply the tools.

And some days, that tool is a thought record. Other days, it's a margarita, a meltdown, or a very long nap under a weighted blanket. Progress isn't linear. It spirals. When it feels like you're circling the same lesson again, don't panic—you're just leveling up.

> *"Resilience is knowing that you are the only one that has the power and the responsibility to pick yourself up."*
> — Mary Holloway[29]

You didn't miss the point by needing help more than once. You've simply joined the club of everyone trying to keep it together while the world shape-shifts hourly.

---

29 Holloway, Mary. The Complete Idiot's Guide to Self-Esteem. New York: Alpha Books, 1999.

FINANCIAL RESILIENCE WITHOUT THE HUSTLE GOSPEL

Let's talk money. Not the kind that buys jet skis (although, yes, happiness can be leased at 45 miles per hour), but the kind that gives you options. Financial stability isn't about becoming rich. It's about insulating your mental health from the chaos of the economy. You don't need to become a crypto bro, flip houses, or start an Etsy for artisanal depression candles. But you do need a plan.

» Reduce unnecessary expenses that are really just mood band-aids.
» Build an emergency fund—even if it's small.
» Diversify your income if possible. Multiple income streams = psychological leverage.
» Don't outsource all your financial decision-making to apps and influencers. Learn the basics yourself.

Money doesn't buy happiness. But a late bill during a panic attack is a whole different flavor of hell. Stability matters. Financial resilience is emotional resilience with receipts. Also, normalize being bad at money in your twenties. Or thirties. Or any decade where the world was on fire (see: all of them). The goal isn't perfection. It's progress. And enough leftover cash for the occasional overpriced coffee that makes you feel alive.

EMOTIONAL RESILIENCE MEANS YOU'RE ALLOWED TO FEEL THINGS

Contrary to every productivity guru on the Internet, resilience is not "feeling nothing." It's feeling deeply, then responding wisely. It's getting the news that your department is being replaced by ChatGPT 8.0 and not immediately selling everything you own to start a goat farm in Montana (though, to be fair, I'd read that memoir). You don't have to stay calm. You don't have to be stoic. You just need to respond instead of react. This is where the mindfulness stuff—yes, even the Still Mode from Chapter 8—starts paying off. You become someone who can feel scared, sad, anxious, or overwhelmed … and still make a phone call, feed the kids, or go on that sad little walk anyway. You gain capacity. And with that capacity comes agency. And with that agency comes power. And just like that, you're no longer just surviving. You're steering.

> *"Emotional resilience is not about resisting life's storms. It's about learning how to dance in the rain, scream into a pillow, and keep going anyway."*
> — Probably you, after this book

CONNECTION: THE REAL INSURANCE POLICY

You want a real prepper strategy? Build a community. No, not a cult (unless the robes are really cool). I mean actual, vulnerable, mutually supportive relationships. Friends. Partners. Colleagues. Family members you don't have to mute on holidays. Connection is what keeps your nervous system from collapsing under the weight of modern life. We are biologically wired to co-regulate with others. Isolation, by contrast, is a slow death sentence, emotionally and sometimes literally. Text someone. Call someone. Start a group chat that isn't about memes or HOA drama. Find your people and invest in them. When everything else breaks, human connection is the backup generator. And if you're someone who struggles to make or keep friends—congratulations, you're not alone. Making adult friendships is hard, awkward, and emotionally equivalent to online dating for platonic soulmates. Start small. Invite someone to walk. Share your weird thoughts. Be brave enough to follow up.

THE BOOK WAS NEVER ABOUT JUST "STAYING SANE"

Let's be honest. This book was not just about staying sane while robots eat your job. That was the hook. The headline. The pitch. But the real mission? It's been about upgrading your inner operating system. We've been building:

> » A brain that doesn't catastrophize every notification
> » A nervous system that doesn't go DEFCON 1 at every email
> » A lifestyle that values meaning over metrics
> » A mindset that can bend without breaking

And you've been part of it the whole time. You've "un-doomscrolled" your brain. Rebranded your narrator. Outrun your dread. Sat in your stillness. Questioned your coping. And maybe—just maybe—glimpsed what it's like to feel like a human again instead of an overwhelmed algorithm with a caffeine dependency. You did that.

> *"The real question is not whether machines think, but whether men do."*
>
> — **B.F. Skinner**[30]

---

30 Skinner, B. F. Contingencies of Reinforcement: A Theoretical Analysis. New York: Appleton-Century-Crofts, 1969.

FINAL THOUGHT: YOU DON'T HAVE TO BE A SUPERHUMAN. JUST A HUMAN WHO TRIES.

Perfection is a prison. Resilience is a practice.

As you move forward, don't make a checklist of ways to "fix" yourself. Just pick one thing, one tool, one shift, and apply it. Messily. Repeatedly. Badly, even. Because the world doesn't need more perfectionists. It needs people who are present. Awake and capable of saying, "This is hard—and I'm still here." Resilience isn't about being untouched by struggle. It's about coming through the fire a little smoky, a little singed, but still standing. You can do hard things. You are resilient. You are capable. And you are human. That's how we stay sane while the robots eat our jobs. That's how we begin. That's how we continue to upgrade. You're not a machine, but you are miraculous. You glitch. You adapt. You carry on.

You're not finished. You're just getting started.

ABOUT THE AUTHOR

Angelo Alfano is a psychiatric and family nurse practitioner, writer, and clinician specializing in mental health, addiction, and resilience in the age of automation. A Yale and Johns Hopkins graduate, his work focuses on helping individuals and organizations navigate burnout, adaptation, and purpose in an AI-driven world. When he's not writing or practicing psychiatry, Angelo is restoring a regenerative homestead in Northern California with his wife and children — raising fruit trees, chickens, and a healthy dose of perspective

For more information or to contact the author, visit
AngeloJohnAlfano.com

www.ingramcontent.com/pod-product-compliance
Lightning Source LLC
Chambersburg PA
CBHW070733030726

47601CB00001B/7